Ten Wriggly, Wiggly Caterpillars

LITTLE TIGER

LONDON

10

Ten crunching caterpillars, in the bright sunshine.

One fell asleep,
so that left...

9

Nine speedy caterpillars, thought they might be late.

One was too **slow**

so that left...

8

Eight munching caterpillars,
all in **cRunChing** heaven!

One got a **tummy ache,**

so that left...

Seven clever caterpillars, **creeping** through some sticks.

One got **stuck,** so that left...

6

Six singing caterpillars, **glad** to be alive.

One stayed to **sing**,
so that left...

Five brave caterpillars, going to **explore**.

One got lost,
so that left...

4

Four **daring** caterpillars, inching up a tree.

One fell off,
so that left...

One got **soaked**,
so that left...

2

Two happy caterpillars, having so much **fun**.

One got **tired**,
so that left...

1

One **sad** caterpillar, all on his own,

when all of a **sudden**
there were...

10

Ten bright and beautiful, pretty butterflies,

spreading their wings,
and flitting through the skies!